WITHDRAWN

The *Untold Story* of Washington's *Surprise Attack*

The Daring Crossing of the Delaware River

by Danny Kravitz

Content Adviser: Mark Sirak
Historian
Washington Crossing State Park
Titusville, New Jersey

COMPASS POINT BOOKS
a capstone imprint

Compass Point Books are published by Capstone,
1710 Roe Crest Drive, North Mankato, Minnesota 56003
www.capstonepub.com

Editorial Credits
Jennifer Huston, editor; Heidi Thompson, designer;
Eric Gohl, media researcher; Laura Manthe, production specialist;
Kathleen Baxter, library consultant

Photo Credits
Alamy: North Wind Picture Archives, 27, 48, 54; Bridgeman Art Library:
© Look and Learn/Private Collection/James Edwin McConnell, cover, 32;
Courtesy of Army Art Collection, U.S. Army Center of Military History: 41;
Courtesy of Mount Vernon Ladies' Association: 37; Getty Images: American
Stock, 17, Ed Vebell, 35, MPI, 51, Stock Montage, 6, SuperStock, 12, UIG/
Chicago History Museum, 43; Glow Images: Superstock, 45; Granger, NYC:
39; Library of Congress: 20; Newscom: Everett Collection, 47, Picture History,
57, World History Archive, 11; United States Military Academy: Department
of History, 15, 53; Wikimedia: The Metropolitan Museum of Art, 5, Oneam,
18, 23, Thomas Sully, 24; www.historicalimagebank.com, Painting by
Don Troiani: 9

Design Elements: Shutterstock

Library of Congress Cataloging-in-Publication Data
Kravitz, Danny, 1970–
   The Untold Story of Washington's Surprise Attack: The Daring Crossing of
the Delaware River by Danny Kravitz.
     pages cm.—What You Didn't Know About the American Revolution
     Includes bibliographical references and index.
     ISBN 978-0-7565-4973-2 (library binding)
     ISBN 978-0-7565-4977-0 (paperback)
     ISBN 978-0-7565-4981-7 (ebook PDF)
1. Trenton, Battle of, Trenton, N.J., 1776—Juvenile literature. 2. Washington,
George, 1732–1799—Military leadership—Juvenile literature. I. Title.

E241.T7K73 2015
973.4'1092—dc23   2014039560

Printed in the United States of America in Stevens Point, Wisconsin.
092014   008479WZS15

TABLE OF *Contents*

Victory or Death

It is Christmas night 1776. Wind and freezing rain pelt the shores of the Delaware River. General George Washington stands on the Pennsylvania side of the river looking across at New Jersey. Behind him 2,400 frightened but determined American soldiers prepare for whatever awaits them. Washington's trusted commanders—Henry Knox, Nathanael Greene, John Sullivan, and John Glover—stand at his side.

On the other side of the Delaware and about 9 miles (14.5 kilometers) to the southeast, a group of fearsome Hessian soldiers are camped at Trenton, ready to fight for the British. Washington must mount his attack against the Hessians before daybreak. Although the freezing rain and sleet fall harder, he will not allow his troops to turn back.

As the men prepare to cross the river, they load their horses and cannons onto large ferryboats. While the soldiers cross the river, chunks of ice, surging waters, and blustery winds slow their progress. Knox shouts through the raging gales as the weary soldiers strain to hear his orders.

"Victory or death" is the phrase they are all thinking. It's a phrase that carries more truth than any other uttered that day, for if they fail they will surely die as will the fight for American independence.

As Washington and his men row toward the New Jersey shore, the snow blows so wildly that they can barely see. While the crew struggles to paddle across the icy river, Washington scans the horizon looking for the shore. At the moment there is nothing he can do but wait.

Emanuel Leutze's famous painting *Washington Crossing the Delaware* shows the men struggling to break through the ice as they cross to the New Jersey side of the river.

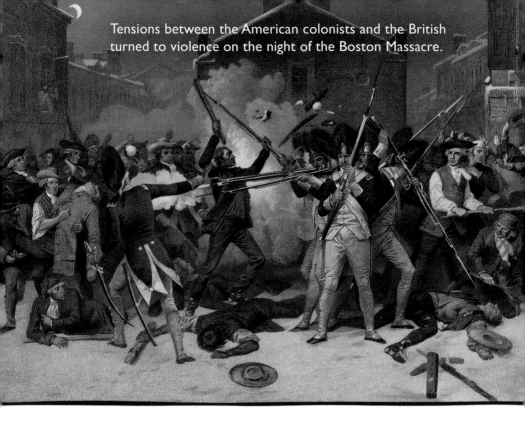

Tensions between the American colonists and the British turned to violence on the night of the Boston Massacre.

Turmoil in the Colonies

In the late 1760s the American Colonies were still part of the British Empire. But the Americans were unhappy with how they were being treated under British rule. In particular they believed that the taxes being forced upon them without their consent were unfair. They demonstrated their unhappiness with protests and acts of defiance.

England's King George III sent troops to Boston in October 1768 to stop the protests and protect the tax collectors. But the presence of British troops only fueled the anger of the colonists. Their resentment boiled over on the night of March 5, 1770, with an incident known as the Boston Massacre. During a protest British soldiers shot 11 Americans and killed five when an argument broke out between the two groups.

More protests soon followed, including the Boston Tea Party on December 16, 1773. By 1774 the flames of the American Revolution began to grow higher. That September representatives from 12 of the 13 colonies (Georgia did not take part) met at the First Continental Congress in Philadelphia. They decided that the British laws were unconstitutional and that they should prepare to fight for their rights. The following year the Second Continental Congress decided that a great general was needed to lead the colonies in their resistance. They chose George Washington.

George Washington

Born in 1732 in Westmoreland County, Virginia, George Washington became a land surveyor before joining the Virginia militia and helping the British win the French and Indian War (1754–1763).

After the war Washington returned home and married a wealthy widow named Martha Dandridge Custis. He spent his time managing his family's estates, hunting, and living a comfortable life as a gentleman farmer and one of Virginia's wealthiest men.

Washington was elected to the Continental Congress in 1774 and 1775. He became the leader of the new Continental army in June 1775. He took the position but told Martha that he would be home by fall. It would actually be eight years before he returned to his life on his estate, Mount Vernon.

Beating Back the British

The first shots of the Revolutionary War were fired on April 19, 1775, when British and American soldiers clashed at Lexington and Concord, just outside Boston.

Many colonists had fled from Boston after the British occupied the city. At the time it was standard practice for the colonists to organize militia groups as a means of protection. So when British soldiers attempted to steal supplies from the colonists near Concord, Massachusetts, local militia groups organized an attack and drove them back.

The patriots won these first two battles, which frustrated the British while empowering the colonists and bolstering their

Did You Know?

During the Revolutionary War Germans who fought for the British were referred to as Hessians. The majority of those who served in the war came from the German state of Hesse-Cassel, which is how they got their nickname. But soldiers from other small German states also helped the British.

By renting out its troops, Hesse-Cassel earned more than 10 times the amount of money it made from taxes. This made its soldiers a major export and a valuable source of revenue.

determination. More fighting was inevitable, including the Battle of Bunker Hill in June—the bloodiest clash of the war.

Washington arrived in Boston in July and took command of the men who had armed themselves against the Redcoats. With Washington at the helm, by mid-March 1776, they not only held off a British advance, they also forced the Redcoats to leave without damaging the city.

Most of the fighting in the Battle of Bunker Hill actually took place at nearby Breed's Hill.

CHAPTER *Two*

The War Is Far From Over

After driving the British from Boston, Washington was hailed as a hero. The *New York Constitutional Gazette* wrote "the British were completely disgraced." But Washington felt that he had lost an opportunity to destroy the British Army. Soon enough he would have to face them again, and the next time they would have more troops. They would also be even more determined to defeat the patriots.

Washington believed that the British would attack New York City, so by April, the Continental army was on its way there. With the help of the persistent patriots and Henry Knox, who traveled more than 700 miles (1,127 km) to retrieve additional artillery, Washington had saved Boston. But now he needed to save his country from a larger, more determined British force.

George Washington received a warm welcome in Boston after the British were forced out following an 11-month siege.

The British Come Back Stronger

After leaving Boston, General William Howe and the British Army retreated to Nova Scotia, a peninsula in Canada, 400 miles (644 km) northeast of Boston. There Howe planned his next move and met up with soldiers arriving from Europe. These new troops would increase the size of the British Army to more than 30,000 soldiers—one of the largest armies ever assembled on North American soil. They included Hessian soldiers as well as British troops under the command of Admiral Lord Richard Howe, General William Howe's brother.

A massive fleet of British warships arrived in New York in late June 1776.

Washington arrived in New York City in mid-April and situated his soldiers in Manhattan and the surrounding areas. With roughly 19,000 soldiers under his command, he hoped to defend the city as he had Boston. He had them build fortifications on the southern end of Manhattan Island. They also built fortifications in Brooklyn Heights and on Long Island.

As they prepared to defend the city, all Washington and his troops could do was wait for the British. When they finally arrived in late June, it was an alarming site to behold. As the British warships neared the coast of New York, their white sails and wooden hulls appeared on the horizon one after the other. The sheer size and strength of the massive armada sailing toward New York was completely unnerving to the Americans.

Not only was the number of ships staggering, but there were more cannons on just a handful of Howe's warships than Washington

had set up to defend all of Manhattan.

Howe arrived on Staten Island on July 2 with 10,000 British and Hessian soldiers. His brother was expected to arrive soon after with even more troops. Two days later on July 4, 1776, the Continental Congress approved the Declaration of Independence. Fed up with British rule, the 13 American colonies boldly declared themselves independent from Great Britain.

In the eyes of the British, by proclaiming their independence from England, the Americans had committed treason—a crime punishable by death. But the colonists had changed the nature of the war. No longer were they fighting over taxes. No longer were they simply defending their property. They were trying to create their own country. With the announcement of the Declaration of Independence, the conflict had become a true revolution.

The British Take New York

By early August a total of 400 British ships with more than 30,000 men had landed at Staten Island. That was almost the same as the entire population of Philadelphia, which was America's largest city at the time.

On July 14 the Howe brothers had sent a letter addressed to George Washington offering to pardon his treasonous behavior. They were hoping to avoid further fighting and bring the Americans back under England's rule. Washington's aide Joseph Reed refused to accept the letter.

Washington eventually agreed to meet with Colonel James Paterson, an assistant to General Howe. But Washington pointed out that the Howes had no authority to negotiate terms between the two countries. As for the pardon, Washington said that it was not needed because the Americans had done nothing wrong. Upon news of the meeting, General Howe reported back to officials in Parliament that there would be no chance of convincing Washington or the Americans to return to British rule.

As a result just before dawn on August 22, the British began their invasion of New York City. With 4,000 troops on transport boats, British Generals Charles Cornwallis and Henry Clinton began leading men from Staten Island to Gravesend Bay on the southern tip of Long Island.

General Howe's forces defeated Washington and his troops on August 27 in what became known as the Battle of Long Island. The Americans made the mistake of leaving a single road unguarded and were soon outsmarted and overpowered by Howe's surprise attack. Washington lost many men, but under cover of fog and darkness, he was able to evacuate his troops and escape across the East River back into Manhattan.

What followed during the next three months was a disaster for Washington and his troops. Losing all but one small skirmish from August through November, they failed to defend New York City and were pushed out of Manhattan by British forces.

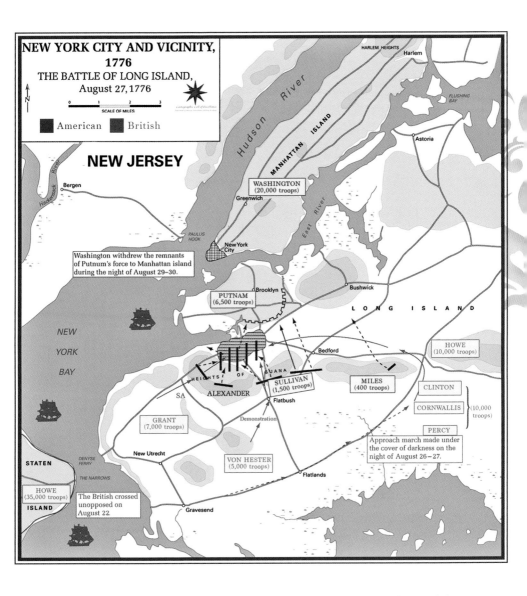

NEW YORK CITY AND VICINITY, 1776

THE BATTLE OF LONG ISLAND, August 27, 1776

SCALE OF MILES
0 1 2 3

■ American ■ British

NEW JERSEY

Hudson River

MANHATTAN ISLAND

East River

HARLEM HEIGHTS
Harlem

FLUSHING BAY

Astoria

Bergen

WASHINGTON (20,000 troops)

Greenwich

PAULUS HOOK

New York City

Washington withdrew the remnants of Putnum's force to Manhattan island during the night of August 29–30.

PUTNAM (6,500 troops)

Brooklyn

Bushwick

LONG ISLAND

HOWE (10,000 troops)

NEW YORK BAY

HEIGHTS OF GUANA

ALEXANDER

SA

SULLIVAN (1,500 troops)

Flatbush

Bedford

MILES (400 troops)

CLINTON

CORNWALLIS (10,000 troops)

GRANT (7,000 troops)

Demonstration

PERCY

Approach march made under the cover of darkness on the night of August 26–27.

New Utrecht

VON HESTER (5,000 troops)

STATEN ISLAND

DENYSE FERRY

THE NARROWS

Flatlands

HOWE (35,000 troops)

The British crossed unopposed on August 22

Gravesend

"This was the first time in my life that I had witnessed the awful scene of a battle, when man was engaged to destroy his fellow-man. I well remember my sensations on the occasion, for ... very hardly could I bring my mind to be willing to attempt the life of a fellow-creature."

—American Colonel Benjamin Tallmadge describing his experience during the Battle of Long Island

Running from the Redcoats

Washington's army then retreated farther north from lower Manhattan. Howe defeated the Americans once again on September 15 when he led five warships up the East River and landed forces at Kip's Bay on Manhattan Island. Washington was so frustrated during the battle that he charged into the fighting, trying to motivate his retreating men and narrowly avoided being killed or captured himself.

The next day Washington and his men retreated north again to Harlem Heights and won a small battle there. Washington had strategized a clever maneuver that trapped the British, who eventually withdrew. Even so, Washington—who feared being surrounded and trapped—was forced to move most of his troops

even farther north to White Plains, New York.

Although the American victory at Harlem Heights boosted morale, overall the New York campaign was a dismal failure for the Continental army. Washington had left behind 2,000

The Battle of Harlem Heights was the only skirmish the Americans won for several months in late 1776.

men to hold Fort Washington on the northern end of Manhattan Island and later sent about 1,000 reinforcements there. But on November 16, 1776, about 5,000 Redcoats and 3,000 Hessians stormed the fort. The Americans offered stiff resistance, but when the smoke cleared, the surviving patriots were captured.

Despite Washington's successes in Boston only months earlier, he was now at risk of total defeat. Winter was fast approaching and there was nothing to do but run from the Redcoats.

CHAPTER *Three*

The Retreat

In late November Washington and his battered troops were retreating south through New Jersey. Rain left the roads thick with mud, and the men were so poorly equipped that many were making the retreat barefoot or with rags wrapped

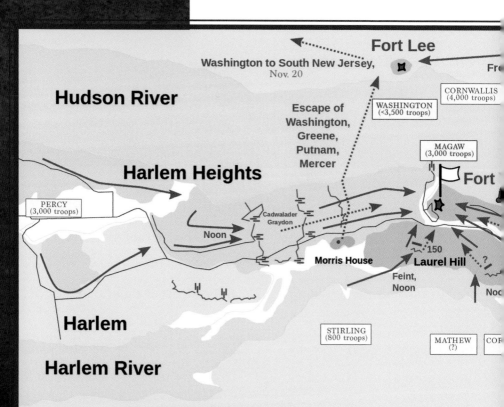

Washington to South New Jersey, Nov. 20

Fort Lee

Hudson River

Escape of Washington, Greene, Putnam, Mercer

WASHINGTON (<3,500 troops)

CORNWALLIS (4,000 troops)

Fr

Harlem Heights

MAGAW (3,000 troops)

Fort

PERCY (3,000 troops)

Noon

Cadwalader Graydon

Morris House

150

Laurel Hill

Feint, Noon

No

Harlem

STIRLING (800 troops)

MATHEW (?)

COF

Harlem River

around their feet. Having to brave the cold, rainy weather, one soldier wrote, "The sufferings we endured are beyond description."

By this time Washington only had about 3,500 men with him. After losing the Battle of White Plains, he had left 6,000 troops under General Charles Lee and 4,000 with General William Heath in New England to prevent British advances. Even with his army battered and bruised, Washington still carried himself with an air of confidence. But inwardly he was very concerned. He sent a letter to General Lee in New York asking for help. Some of his men were without tents and other equipment because, after being warned of a British advance, the patriots had abandoned Fort Lee on November 20, leaving much of their supplies behind. Washington knew that to face the British forces under these conditions would mean certain defeat.

Washington also feared that many of his men would soon leave because some enlistments were due to expire on December 1. Washington sent requests for troops from Philadelphia and New Jersey, but he received no reassurance that any would come.

Battle of Fort Washington
November 16, 1776

- United States
- Great Britain
- Battery

0 (km) 0.75
0 (mi) 0.5

...th,
...0

...hington
...bardment,
07:00

Noon Hessian Battery

Rall

07:00

...S

King's Bridge

KNYPHAUSEN
(4,000 troops)

Thomas Paine, who traveled with the Continental army as an aide, wrote an article called "The Crisis" to describe what Washington and his men were facing. It began with the now famous words, "These are the Times that try men's souls."

Common Sense. Rights of Man

Thomas Paine

After the defeats in New York, many questioned Washington's abilities as the commander of the Continental army. Even Joseph Reed, his closest aide, had lost confidence in him. Reed sent a letter to General Lee suggesting that Washington be replaced. In the letter Reed criticized Washington's leadership and spoke about his uncertainty during the New York campaign.

Meanwhile, many of Washington's men were deserting. Some simply went home, but others joined the British because they were starting to lose faith that the Americans could win the war. The British also knew that Washington and his army were in trouble. Lord Rawdon, a captain in the British Army, wrote, "their army is broken all to pieces … it is well nigh over with them."

Washington arrived in Brunswick, New Jersey, on November 29 with British troops in hot pursuit. General William Alexander Stirling joined him there and brought with him 1,000 soldiers. Many of these men lacked shoes and shirts.

The next day General Howe issued a proclamation to American citizens: Should they pledge their loyalty to England within 60 days, they would receive a pardon. That would allow them to do business and protect their rights as citizens of England. Thousands took him up on the offer.

That same day Washington finally received news from General Lee. But instead of saying that he was on his way to help Washington, the letter said that he hadn't yet left New York.

Then on December 1, just as Washington had feared, 2,000 militiamen headed for home. British and Hessian troops were only hours away from Washington's camp. In desperation, Washington sent a letter to John Hancock, president of the Continental Congress, asking for help. But the Continental Congress and the citizens of Philadelphia were busy preparing to flee the city in case the Redcoats invaded. Having no other choice, Washington led his meager band of roughly 2,500 men to Trenton, New Jersey, about 25 miles (40 km) to the south.

Hot on Washington's Trail

On December 7 Howe and the British forces moved closer to Trenton in pursuit of the Continental army. With growing loyalist support and troops at the ready, Howe thought he might be able to defeat Washington and gain more American land.

When Washington heard of the British advance, he ordered his troops to retreat south across the Delaware River into Pennsylvania. Overnight, under cover of darkness, the soldiers moved horses and artillery onto boats, crossed the river, and then labored again to get them ashore.

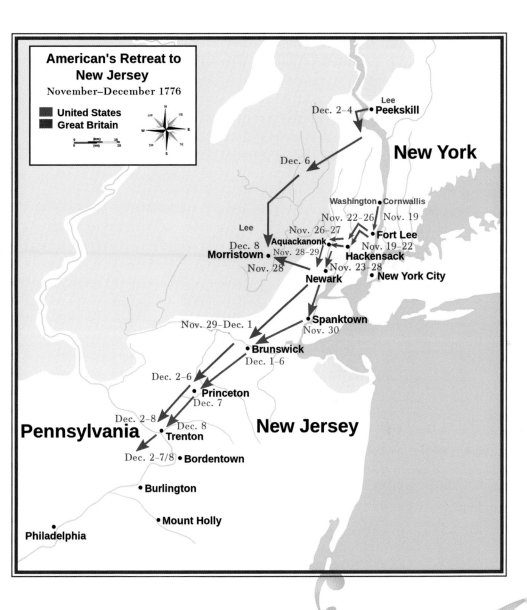

In *The Passage of the Delaware*, artist Thomas Sully portrayed Washington as a calm, decisive leader.

The following day Washington's troops were safely on the Pennsylvania side of the river. But they were a broken mass of men. Exhausted, ill, and without proper clothes or equipment, they were quickly losing hope.

The Continental army stretched out for 25 miles (40 km) along the Pennsylvania side of the Delaware. About 1,000 militiamen arrived from Philadelphia to join them, but their presence provided only a small boost in morale.

Did You Know?

Charles Willson Peale was one of the Philadelphia militiamen who joined Washington's force and saw the dismal state of the army. As he walked the shore of the Delaware, Peale came upon a soldier who was barely clothed, bearded, and so dirty and covered with sores that he didn't recognize him. Then he realized it was his brother.

How Can We Survive?

Washington ordered his army to take or destroy any boats docked for 60–70 miles (97–113 km) along the New Jersey side of the Delaware. He wanted to make sure that the British couldn't use the boats to cross the river and attack. But Washington still worried that the British would bring their own boats. His one hope was that General Lee would arrive with 4,000 soldiers to bolster his position.

But then Washington received news that on December 13 General Lee had been captured. It was a terrible blow to the already defeated morale of the men. And as if that wasn't enough, Washington learned that Congress had fled Philadelphia.

The only good news for Washington was that with the arrival of winter, General Howe had decided to stop fighting until spring. Howe and his soldiers headed north to wait out the winter in the comfort of New York City. But he left some troops stationed at outposts along the way, including a group of Hessians in Trenton.

The General in His Pajamas

In late 1776 General Lee had been moving his troops toward Washington's position. But on the night of December 12, he left his soldiers at their camp and went to a tavern a few miles away. The next morning Lee was captured by the British—while still in his pajamas and slippers!

Like many officers in the Continental army, General Charles Lee had served in the British Army during the French and Indian War.

Washington was unaware of Howe's plans. In fact, Washington was convinced that Howe would attack the moment the river froze. Even after receiving news that Howe had left for New York, Washington continued to fear for his troops.

In the midst of a snowstorm on December 20, General Lee's men (now under the command of General John Sullivan) finally arrived. But when Washington saw them, his heart sank. There were not 4,000 soldiers as he'd hoped but only 2,000. And they were in such bad shape that many of them bloodied the snow with their shoeless feet. General Horatio Gates also arrived from New York that day, but he only brought about 600 soldiers. Adding to Washington's concerns, more enlistments were ending on January 1, which was less than two weeks away. Washington faced the real possibility that a sizable number of his weary troops would simply pack up and go home. Things could not have seemed worse for Washington and the Continental army.

"... your imagination can scarce extend to a situation more distressing than mine—Our only [hope] ... is upon the Speedy Inlistment of a New Army; if this fails us, I think the game will be pretty well up."

—George Washington in a letter to his cousin Lund Washington, December 10–17, 1776

What to Do When All Seems Lost

Washington now had approximately 7,500 men with him, but perhaps as many as 1,500 of them were injured or too sick to fight. Even among the healthy, men were freezing from the brutal winter temperatures and the lack of proper clothing and blankets. The winter was one of the coldest the area had ever experienced.

In the eyes of the British and many Americans, the Continental army was defeated and their fight for independence was all but over. Most believed it was just a matter of time before Washington surrendered.

Despite the weather, the condition of his troops, the lack of support from his countrymen, and the lack of faith in his leadership, Washington was determined to continue the fight. He simply refused to abandon the cause of freedom that so greatly mattered to the future of his country. Most people wondered how long Washington and his Continental army could survive. But the determined Virginian already had a plan in motion.

Did You Know?

It's no secret that Washington was aided by spies during the Revolutionary War. Historians believe that a spy named John Honeyman gave Washington information on the Hessian troops stationed at Trenton. Acting as a double-agent, Honeyman also told the Hessians that the Americans had retreated to Pennsylvania for the winter. As a result, the Hessians let their guard down and Washington took advantage of the opportunity.

CHAPTER *Four*

Washington Goes on the Attack

Washington believed that in order to avoid defeat he needed a bold, unexpected attack. An aggressive move would surprise the enemy and give Americans hope that they could win the war. Defeating the British in the field would also motivate

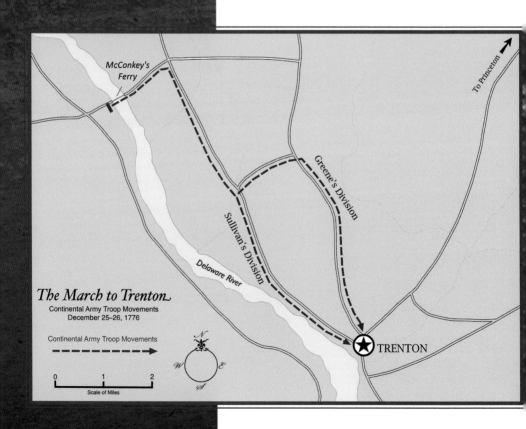

McConkey's Ferry

To Princeton

Greene's Division

Sullivan's Division

Delaware River

TRENTON

The March to Trenton
Continental Army Troop Movements
December 25–26, 1776

Continental Army Troop Movements

0   1   2
Scale of Miles

N
W   E
S

his troops and provide a reason for new soldiers to join the fight. It was something he'd been pondering since his retreat across the Delaware.

To share his ideas and plan the attack, Washington met with a handful of his most trusted men. Despite the horrible condition of the army and the bitterly cold weather, they decided they would cross the Delaware and confront the enemy at Trenton.

Washington's Daring Plan

Washington believed that there were 2,000 to 3,000 enemy troops stationed at Trenton. His daring and complex plan called for the Continental army to cross the Delaware into New Jersey at three different points.

First, General James Ewing would lead 700 militiamen across the river near Trenton. They would also secure a bridge over the Assunpink Creek, which would prevent the enemy from using it as an escape route.

Next, General John Cadwalader and Joseph Reed would lead 1,500 men across the river at Bristol, Pennsylvania, about 10 miles (16 km) southwest of Trenton.

Finally, Washington's men would cross at McConkey's Ferry, about 9 miles (14 km) north of General Ewing's group. Washington's party would split into two groups for their approach to Trenton. One would travel close to the river and the other would swing around and approach from the north.

Washington planned to start the assault on Trenton an hour before daybreak on December 26. That would give the men an hour of darkness to close in on the enemy before sunrise. But it also meant they would have to arrive at Trenton by 5:00 a.m.

As Christmas day dawned, a winter storm was approaching. By nighttime brutal cold, blustery winds, freezing rain, and heavy snow threatened to hinder Washington's plan.

In the early afternoon, Washington left his headquarters to join his troops, and by 2:00 p.m. the men were making their way to the river. Each soldier had with him food for three days and 60 rounds of ammunition. None of them knew where they were going or what awaited them. The important mission was such a secret that Washington ordered total silence among his troops.

That night Washington learned that the men in Bristol were unable to cross because large chunks of ice were clogging the river. Washington sent a note to Cadwalader that said, "If you can do nothing real, at least create as great a diversion as possible."

By early evening on Christmas night 1776, about 2,400 American troops began crossing the Delaware River.

The Crossing of the Delaware

By nightfall when Washington's men arrived at McConkey's Ferry, a steady rain was falling. Soon the rain turned to hail and then snow. In the howling winds, Henry Knox barked out orders, directing the men to move the 18 cannons and 50-plus horses onto the large, flat-bottomed boats.

While crossing the river, the men dug their oars into the water as they struggled to navigate the treacherous, icy water. The strong currents threatened to push the boats off course.

Washington and the men who had already crossed watched with growing fear as the remaining troops struggled to reach the New Jersey side. By the time all the soldiers, horses, and cannons were across the river, the mission was already three hours behind schedule and dawn was fast approaching.

Because of the storm, Washington knew he'd lost his chance for a surprise attack under the cover of darkness. But if he abandoned the plan at this point, he knew the Hessians would see them and launch a counterattack. He had no other choice but to move ahead with the attack.

Washington had no idea that as he was deciding to go forth, the other two arms of his three-pronged attack had already failed. The storm had beaten back both Ewing and Cadwalader before they and their men could complete the crossings at

Trenton and Bristol. Both men had called off their attacks. Even so, Washington and his men marched toward Trenton.

"... the wind blew very hard and there was much rain and sleet ... there was so much floating ice in the River that we had the greatest difficulty [getting] over again, and some of our men did not get over that night."

—Captain Thomas Rodney, from his diary entry December 25, 1776

Washington shivered in the cold as his men labored to row their boats across the Delaware River.

Five miles (8 km) after crossing the Delaware, Washington split his troops into two groups. He and Nathanael Greene led a group north of Trenton to Pennington Road, while John Sullivan's group took River Road to make their approach from the west.

By the time the two groups finally reached Trenton, the sun had already risen. Even so, Washington had his men prepare to attack.

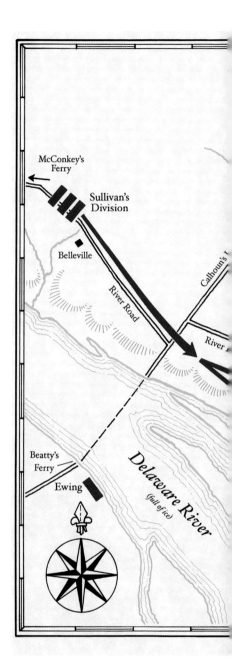

On Christmas day in seventy-six
Our ragged troops with bayonets fixed
For Trenton marched away.
The Delaware see! the boats below!
The light obscured by hail and snow!
But no signs of dismay ...

In silent march we passed the night,
Each soldier panting for the fight,
Though quite benumbed with frost.
Greene, on the left, at six began.
The right was led by Sullivan
Who ne'er a moment lost.

—Excerpt from "Battle of Trenton"

Battle of Trenton

DECEMBER 25–26, 1776

The March to Trenton

Continental Army

McConkey's Ferry

Greene's Division

Delaware River

Pennington Road

Sullivan's Division

River Road

Trenton

0   1   2   Scale of Miles

Princeton Road

Greene's Division

Washington

Stephen

Stirling

Fermoy

Pennington Road

Mercer

Petty's Run

apple orchard

Rall & Lossberg Regts. surrender

King St.

Queen St.

Ⓐ

St. Clair

Petty's Run

Ⓒ

④

Fourth St.

⑤

Third St.

Knyphausen Regt. surrenders

Ⓑ

⑦

Ⓓ

③

Second St.

❽

Ⓔ

❶

Front St.

❷'

⑥

⑨

Sargent

Assunpink Bridge

Douglass house

Assunpink Creek

Glover

battery

Bordentown Road

noncombatants and some Hessians escape

— Key —

Ⓐ Rall's HQ
Ⓑ Rall Regt.
Ⓒ Lossberg Regt.
Ⓓ Knyphausen Regt.
❶ Courthouse
❷ Steel Works
❸ Presbyterian Church
④ St. Michael's Church
⑤ Friends Meeting House
⑥ John Barnes house
⑦ Abraham Hunt house
❽ Old Stone Barracks
⑨ Mahlon Stacy's Mill

American brig. — ▬

artillery — ⚏

Hessian regt. — ▬

Hessian outposts - ○ ○ ○

0   ¼   ½

Scale of Miles

Rick Britton

George Washington's
MOUNT VERNON

The Attack

Trenton was a small village in 1776, with just a church, a marketplace, a few mills, and two stone barracks that were built during the French and Indian War. Just outside of town, a small bridge crossed the Assunpink Creek. When Washington and his troops arrived, there were only 1,500 Hessian soldiers stationed there—not the 3,000 Washington originally thought.

Colonel Johann Gottlieb Rall, commander of the Hessian troops at Trenton, received word on Christmas day that the Americans might attack late in the afternoon. Just after dusk a small patrol of Americans shot at some of

the Hessians on the outskirts of town and then quickly retreated. Rall assumed that was the attack he'd been warned about, so he went to a small Christmas gathering before heading off to bed for the night. Rall's misguided assumption would prove lucky for Washington.

As the Continental army reached Trenton just after 8:00 a.m. on December 26, heavy snow swirled in the howling winds. The soldiers struggled just to see a few feet ahead of themselves. Nevertheless, Washington did not postpone the attack.

Early on the morning of December 26, a company of New York artillerymen prepared to give the Hessians in Trenton the surprise of a lifetime.

Some of the Americans circled around the village to cut off escape routes. Greene and his men dashed out of the woods and ran through a field toward Trenton, firing at the Hessians positioned there. The Hessians shot back as they retreated. They also tried to set up a cannon, but a group of patriots charged them, seized the cannon, and used it against the Germans.

Knox began firing his cannons, which were set up on the edge of town and on King and Queen Streets. The violent blasts quickly cleared the streets of Hessian soldiers. Some of the Hessians ran for the side streets, but they were met by Sullivan's men and the bayonets at the end of their muskets. Violent, hand-to-hand combat ensued, and the fresh, clean snow was soon speckled with the blood of men struggling for their lives.

Awakened by the assault, Colonel Rall desperately tried to organize his men amidst the chaos of gunshots, smoke, wind, and blinding snow. But he and

Washington's daring crossing of the Delaware River paid off with an impressive victory at the Battle of Trenton.

his soldiers were overwhelmed by the surprise attack. With no other choice but to retreat, he ordered his men to an apple orchard on the southeast end of town.

No sooner had he given this order when a musket ball knocked him from his horse. Rall was carried back to his quarters, where he died from his wound.

When the retreating Hessians arrived at the orchard, they found even more American soldiers waiting for them. Surrounded, the Hessians had no choice but to admit defeat. They dropped their weapons, raised their arms, and surrendered.

The Joy of Victory

A young officer named James Wilkinson later recalled delivering the news of the Hessian surrender to Washington. On receiving the message Washington took him by the hand and said, "Major Wilkinson … this is a glorious day for our country."

In a letter to John Hancock on December 27, Washington reported that "our Loss is very trifling indeed, only two Officers and one or two privates

Did You Know?

Captain William Washington, George Washington's cousin, led the group who captured the cannon from the Hessians during the Battle of Trenton. He was one of the Americans wounded in the battle. James Monroe, who would later become the fifth president of the United States, was also seriously wounded at Trenton.

This painting shows Colonel Rall clutching a wound that would prove fatal as he gives his sword to Washington in surrender. But historians now believe that because Rall was gravely wounded in the battle, it was actually his second in command who surrendered.

wounded." Two patriots had also frozen to death during the march to Trenton. On the other hand, 21 Hessians were dead, 90 were injured, and another 900 were captured. An additional 500 Hessians had escaped out of town over the Assunpink Bridge.

After securing the prisoners, cannons, and other supplies they had seized, Washington's men marched through the night. For the second time in two days, they crossed the Delaware, at times jumping up and down to shake off the ice forming on the bottom of the boats. They finally returned to camp in Pennsylvania in the early morning hours of December 27.

CHAPTER Six

It's Not Over Yet

After the Battle of Trenton, there was a renewed sense of hope, pride, and morale among the soldiers and officers. They had achieved something extraordinary, and they knew it. Washington addressed his men and praised them for their "spirited and gallant behavior." He even promised them a reward for all the horses, cannons, and supplies that were captured.

Newspapers wrote of the surprise attack and of the capture of men and supplies. As news of the victory spread,

Did You *Know?*

John Hancock wrote to Washington on January 1, 1777, praising his ability to inspire his men and acknowledging his accomplishment despite the "broken" state of his army. Calling his victory "extraordinary," he wrote on behalf of the Continental Congress, "to your Wisdom and Conduct, the United States are indebted for the late Success of their Arms."

When Washington and his men crossed to the New Jersey side of the Delaware on December 30, the conditions were almost as brutal as they had been when they crossed a few days earlier.

patriots everywhere—including prisoners of the British—were suddenly excited by an idea foreign to them since Washington's early success in Boston: The Americans just might win this war.

Washington Crosses the Delaware Again

Washington knew that in addition to a British retaliation, his army was still at risk of falling apart when enlistments came to an end on December 31. So he decided to take advantage of the enthusiasm of his men by immediately mounting another attack.

On December 30 Washington crossed the Delaware into New Jersey for a second time. His troops followed the next day. The partially frozen river proved just as difficult to navigate as it had just days earlier. In some places the ice was thick enough to support the weight of soldiers. At others, boats were still needed. There was also nearly a foot of fresh snow on the ground. But they made it across again, this time with 40 cannons plus men and horses.

Arriving back in Trenton Washington settled his troops on a ridge that was protected by the Assunpink Creek on one side and woods on the other. Then he spent December 31 pleading with his men to re-enlist. Addressing them from atop his horse, he asked those in line to step forward if they were willing to re-enlist. None did. Again he pleaded with them, stating that he understood they had already done more than could be asked of them. He said he knew that they had "worn [themselves] out with fatigues and hardships," but their country needed them and all that was important to them was at risk. He assured them: "If you will consent to stay only one month longer, you will render that service to the cause of liberty and to your country which you probably never can do under any other circumstances. The present is … the crisis, which is to decide our destiny."

Despite all they had endured, the men were moved by Washington's words. They understood what was as stake. And Washington had shown that while the price of freedom was great, he himself was willing to sacrifice to achieve it. After a few tense moments, the men began to step forward from the line.

Did You Know?

Washington also awarded his men extra money for re-enlisting. Congress gladly agreed since he had removed their doubts concerning his leadership and had given them renewed hope for success.

Washington and his troops would endure six more brutal winters before the end of the war.

"...[although] desirous as others to return home
I engaged to Stay that time & made every exertion
in my power to make as many of the Soldiers stay
with me as I could & quite a number did engage
with me who otherwise would have went home."

—Elisha Bostwick of the Seventh Connecticut Regiment

British General
Charles Cornwallis

What Will the British Do?

Trenton had been an unexpected loss for the British. Set on righting that military misstep, British General Charles Cornwallis and 8,000 soldiers arrived in Princeton, New Jersey, on January 1, 1777. He left some of his men there and proceeded toward Trenton to mount an attack on Washington.

On the way to Trenton, Cornwallis was greeted by 1,000 American troops sent to delay the British arrival in Trenton. The groups exchanged musket and rifle fire, and the Americans retreated out of town and across Assunpink Creek. There Henry Knox and his artillery force held off the British as they tried three times to break the American position and cross the bridge. At nightfall Cornwallis decided to halt his attacks until the morning. That would prove to be a costly mistake.

That night the British slept on the cold, snow-covered ground. They didn't even burn campfires so they could keep an eye on the Americans across the creek.

While they slept, Washington and more than 5,000 of his men snuck out of their camp. A small force stayed behind to keep the campfires burning and make noise to trick the British into thinking the entire army was still there.

At dawn Cornwallis awoke to find that the Americans were gone. Cornwallis thought that Washington may have escaped by crossing the Delaware River back into Pennsylvania. But Washington had other plans.

Instead of going south, Washington and his soldiers snuck north along back roads to mount another surprise attack on the troops Cornwallis had left in Princeton. They marched through the night, keeping silent and struggling along the icy trails and thick wooded terrain.

Washington ordered Generals John Sullivan and Nathanael Greene to lead their men in opposite directions—Sullivan would come in from the east, Greene from the west. Washington also dispatched General Hugh Mercer and 300 men to destroy a bridge west of Princeton to prevent an enemy retreat. As the men arrived at the bridge at dawn on January 3, they encountered Colonel Charles Mawhood's troops who were on their way to Trenton to help Cornwallis' men. Greene's men soon came upon British soldiers as well.

The Redcoats were taken completely by surprise. They simply couldn't believe that such a large American force was attacking them. They still thought the Continental army was camped in Trenton.

The deadly fighting began immediately and soon spilled

Washington's encouraging words inspired his troops to fight harder, which turned the battle in their favor.

out onto a large farm and apple orchard owned by William Clark. Although the British were outnumbered five to one, the fighting was so fierce that even Washington, Greene, and Cadwalader fought on the front lines.

"Washington appeared in front of the American army, riding towards those of us who were retreating, and exclaimed, 'Parade with us, my brave fellows! There is but a handful of the enemy, and we will have them directly.'"

—"Battle of Princeton," written by Sergeant "R"

Within 15 minutes the British had been overtaken and were making a hasty retreat toward Trenton. At first the Americans pursued them, with Washington cheering and racing after them on his horse. But satisfied with his victory, he soon stopped and ordered a halt to the chase.

Washington estimated that about 30 Americans died during the Battle of Princeton. The losses were much higher for British and Hessians with about 250 men killed and 300 taken prisoner. It was another incredible success for the Americans.

Encouraged by these two victories, Washington considered marching north to Brunswick to destroy British supplies stored there. He felt it could effectively end the war. But his officers warned him that his men did not have the strength for another 20-mile (32-km) march followed by a third battle. They feared they would lose all that had been gained. In the end they convinced Washington to hold off. As determined as he was to end the war, peace would not come for six more years.

The Mercer Oak

General Hugh Mercer was a doctor from Virginia and a close comrade of George Washington. During the Battle of Princeton, he was forced to jump to the ground and fight with his sword after his horse was stabbed with a bayonet. Mercer was fatally stabbed seven times with a bayonet. He died nine days later. An oak tree where he supposedly rested while his men continued the assault became known as the Mercer Oak.

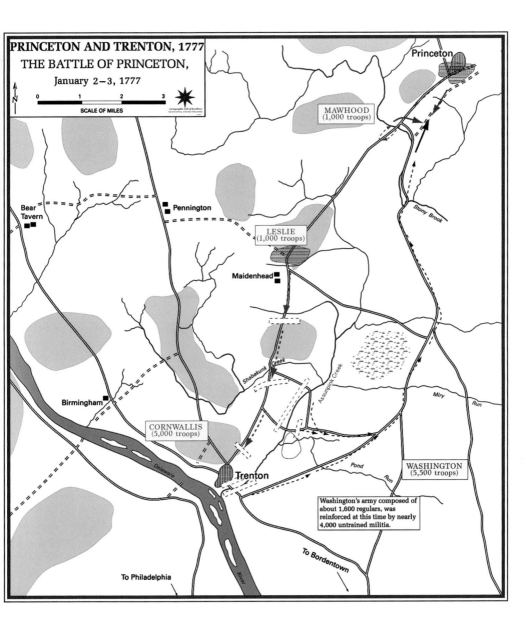

PRINCETON AND TRENTON, 1777
THE BATTLE OF PRINCETON,
January 2–3, 1777

0   1   2   3
SCALE OF MILES

N

Princeton

MAWHOOD
(1,000 troops)

Stony Brook

Bear
Tavern

Pennington

LESLIE
(1,000 troops)

Maidenhead

Shabakunk Creek

Assunpink Creek

Birmingham

CORNWALLIS
(5,000 troops)

Miry
Run

Delaware

Trenton

Pond
Run

WASHINGTON
(5,500 troops)

Washington's army composed of
about 1,600 regulars, was
reinforced at this time by nearly
4,000 untrained militia.

To Bordentown

To Philadelphia

River

*"The British were unable to resist this attack, and retreated
into the College, where they thought themselves safe. Our
army was there in an instant, and cannon were planted
before the door, and after two or three discharges a white
flag appeared in the window, and the British surrendered."*

—"Battle of Princeton," written by Sergeant "R"

53

CHAPTER
Seven

The Tide Has Turned

At Trenton and Princeton, the Continental army had handily defeated the British. For the first time in the war, they had outmaneuvered and outfought

Washington led his troops to another much-needed victory at the Battle of Princeton.

a better-equipped and more experienced enemy in the field. These victories, particularly the one at Trenton, had a profound effect on the outcome of the war.

Suddenly the morale of the patriots was revitalized. Congress and the people now believed in Washington's leadership and threw their support behind him. An influx of new soldiers enlisted.

As for the British, their losses at Trenton and Princeton created new worries as well as a new respect for the Continental army. They also began to doubt whether they could easily win the war.

Perhaps most importantly, other countries soon became involved. As a direct result of Washington's successes at Trenton and Princeton, the Americans received money and military support from France, which proved crucial to winning the war. At the same time, the British were losing Parliament's support for the war and becoming burdened by new conflicts with other European nations.

1777: After Trenton and Princeton

While spending the rest of the winter encamped in Morristown, New Jersey, Washington strengthened his army with new enlistments. He also implemented incentives to keep existing soldiers, including bonuses of money and land. By spring he had roughly 11,000 soldiers and more men were enlisting every day.

After Trenton and Princeton, there were minor skirmishes between the British and some American militia who harassed them throughout the winter in New Jersey. But after Washington's crossings, the conflict broadened. And it carried on for years—initially with the British struggling to hold the North and then targeting the southern states with no real success. Washington continued to win battles and act defensively when necessary to preserve his army.

On October 19, 1781, General Cornwallis, the commander in chief of the British forces, surrendered at Yorktown, Virginia. By January 1782 the British started their withdrawal from the colonies. The war officially ended with the Treaty of Paris in 1783.

In the years that followed, the United States continued to grow as a democratic nation. Congress wrote its own constitution, constructed its various branches, and got on with the business of becoming a great country.

As for Washington, he became the country's first president. His victories at Trenton and Princeton were crucial turning points in America's ultimate defeat of the British in the

Revolutionary War. It has been said that Washington's brilliant determination won the war. Without it the American Revolution may not have survived.

"The achievements of Washington and his little band of compatriots between the 25th of December and the 4th of January, a space of ten days, were the most brilliant of any recorded in the annals of military achievements."

—Frederick the Great, King of Prussia (1740–1786), on the Battles of Trenton and Princeton

Not long after General Cornwallis surrendered to Washington following the Battle of Yorktown, Parliament decided to end the war and let the United States have its freedom and independence.

Timeline

October 1768: British troops arrive in Boston to deal with the colonists' protests and protect British tax collectors.:

March 5, 1770: The Boston Massacre occurs.

December 16, 1773: The Boston Tea Party occurs.

April 19, 1775: British and American soldiers clash at Lexington and Concord; the Revolutionary War officially begins.

July 3, 1775: Washington takes command of the newly formed Continental army at Cambridge, Massachusetts.

March 5, 1776: During the Siege of Boston, Washington sets up cannons overlooking the British position in the city, giving the Americans a powerful advantage.

March 17, 1776: Under General William Howe the British leave Boston after being outsmarted by Washington and his forces.

April 1776: Washington leads his troops to New York City and fortifies lower Manhattan.

July 2, 1776: General Howe arrives on Staten Island, New York, with British and Hessian soldiers.

July 4, 1776: The Continental Congress approves the Declaration of Independence.

August 22, 1776: The British begin their invasion of New York City.

August 27, 1776: General Howe's forces defeat Washington at the Battle of Long Island.

September 15, 1776: Howe defeats the Americans at Kip's Bay in Manhattan.

September 16, 1776: The Americans win a small victory at the Battle of Harlem Heights.

October 28, 1776: The Continental army retreats from the Battle of White Plains.

November 29, 1776:	Washington and his troops retreat to Brunswick, New Jersey.
December 7–8, 1776:	Washington and his troops retreat across the Delaware River into Pennsylvania.
December 25, 1776:	Washington crosses the Delaware into New Jersey to mount an attack on the British forces stationed at Trenton.
December 26, 1776:	Washington attacks and defeats the Hessians at the Battle of Trenton.
December 27, 1776:	Washington leads his victorious troops back across the Delaware to their camp in Pennsylvania.
December 30–31, 1776:	Washington leads his troops across the Delaware into New Jersey to attack the British again.
January 2, 1777:	About 1,000 Continental troops engage the British in a small skirmish near Assunpink Creek. This gives Washington a strategic advantage by delaying the arrival of the British in Trenton until nightfall.
January 3, 1777:	Washington defeats the British at the Battle of Princeton in New Jersey.
January 6, 1777:	The Continental army settles into its winter quarters in Morristown, New Jersey.
October 19, 1781:	General Cornwallis, commander in chief of the British forces, surrenders at Yorktown, Virginia.
January 1782:	The British start their withdrawal from the United States.
September 3, 1783:	The Treaty of Paris is signed; it officially ends the war and acknowledges the United States as an independent nation.

Glossary

armada—a large fleet of ships

barracks—dormlike buildings in which soldiers sleep on a military base

enlistment—the period of time for which one is committed to military service

fortifications—buildings or walls built as military defenses

gentleman farmer—a man who farms mainly for pleasure rather than for profit

Hessian—a German soldier hired by the British

land surveyor—a person whose job is to measure and examine an area of land

loyalist—a colonist who was loyal to Great Britain during the Revolutionary War

militia—a group of volunteer citizens organized to fight but who are not professional soldiers

Parliament—the national legislature of Great Britain

patriot—a person who sided with the American Colonies during the Revolutionary War

strategize—to make a plan for achieving a goal such as a military or political goal

treason—the crime of betraying one's government

Further Reading

Micklos, John, Jr. *Washington's Crossing the Delaware and the Winter at Valley Forge Through Primary Sources.* Berkeley Heights, N.J.: Enslow Publishers, Inc., 2013.

Morey, Allan. *A Timeline History of the Early American Republic.* Minneapolis: Lerner Publications, 2015.

Murphy, Jim. *The Crossing: How George Washington Saved the American Revolution.* New York: Scholastic Press, 2010.

Roberts, Russell. *The Battle of Yorktown.* Hockessin, Del.: Mitchell Lane Publishers, 2012.

Internet Sites

Use FactHound to find Internet sites related to this book. All of the sites on FactHound have been researched by our staff.

Here's all you do:

Visit *www.facthound.com*

Type in this code: 9780756549732

Critical Thinking Using the Common Core

1. Crossing the Delaware on December 26, 1776, was a very risky move for Washington. Using logical reasoning and relevant evidence from the text, write an opinion piece describing why you think Washington took this risk, why it was such an important maneuver, and what might have happened had the mission failed. (Text Types and Purposes)

2. Study the map on page 23. How does it help you understand the text better? What does it tell you about how the war was progressing for the Continental army? (Integration of Knowledge and Ideas)

Source Notes

Page 10, line 4: David G. McCullough. *1776*. New York: Simon & Schuster, 2005, p. 108.

Page 15, callout quote: Benjamin Tallmadge. *Memoir of Col. Benjamin Tallmadge, Prepared by Himself, at the Request of his Children*. New York: Printed by Thomas Holman, 1858, pp. 9–10.

Page 19, col. 1, line 3: William M. Dwyer. *The Day is Ours!: November 1776–January 1777: An Inside View of the Battles of Trenton and Princeton*. New York: Viking Press, 1983, p. 41.

Page 20, fact box, line 5: Thomas Paine. *The Writings of Thomas Paine, Volume 1, Collected and Edited by Moncure Daniel Conway, 1774–1779*. 11 November 2014. http://www.gutenberg.org/files/3741/3741-h/3741-h.htm#link2H_4_0005

Page 21, col. 1, line 23: Henry Steele Commager and Richard B. Morris, eds. *The Spirit of 'Seventy-Six: The Story of the American Revolution as Told by Participants*. New York: Harper & Row, 1967, p. 497.

Page 28, callout quote: Philander D. Chase, ed. *The Papers of George Washington, Revolutionary War Series, vol. 7, 21 October 1776–5 January 1777*. Charlottesville: University Press of Virginia, 1997, pp. 289–292.

Page 33, col. 2, line 20: ibid, p. 439.

Page 35, callout quote: Thomas Rodney. *The Diary of Captain Thomas Rodney*. Wilmington: The Historical Society of Delaware, 1888, p. 23.

Page 36, callout quote: Frank Moore, ed. *Songs and Ballads of the American Revolution*. New York: Appleton & Company, 1855, pp. 150–152.

Page 42, line 9: James Wilkinson. *Memoirs of My Own Times*. Philadelphia: Printed by Abraham Small, 1816, p. 131.

Page 42, line 12: *The Papers of George Washington, Revolutionary War Series, vol. 7, 21 October 1776–5 January 1777*, pp. 454–461.

Page 44, line 6: *The Papers of George Washington, Revolutionary War Series, vol. 7, 21 October 1776–5 January 1777*, pp. 448–449.

Page 44, fact box, line 6: *The Papers of George Washington, Revolutionary War Series, vol. 7, 21 October 1776–5 January 1777*, pp. 505–507.

Page 46, col. 1, line 15: Sergeant R., "The Battle of Princeton." *Pennsylvania Magazine of History and Biography, vol. XX*, 1869, p. 516.

Page 46, col. 2, line 4: "The Battle of Princeton," p. 516.

Page 47, callout quote: Elisha Bostwick, "A Connecticut Soldier Under Washington: Elisha Bostwick's Memoirs of the First Years of the Revolution." Edited by William S. Powell. *William and Mary Quarterly*, Third Series, Vol. 6, No. 1, January 1949, pp. 94–107.

Page 51, callout quote: "The Battle of Princeton," p. 517.

Page 53, callout quote: "The Battle of Princeton," p. 518.

Page 57, callout quote: George Washington Parke Custis and Mary Randolph Custis Lee. *Recollections and Private Memoirs of Washington*. Washington, D.C.: W.H. Moore, 1859, p. 190.

Select Bibliography

Boatner, Mark M, III. *Encyclopedia of the American Revolution.* Mechanicsburg, Pa.: Stackpole Books, 1994.

Bostwick, Elisha. "A Connecticut Soldier Under Washington: Elisha Bostwick's Memoirs of the First Years of the Revolution." Edited by William S. Powell. *William and Mary Quarterly*, Third Series, Vol. 6, No. 1, January 1949: pp. 94–107.

Carbone, Gerald M. *Washington: Lessons in Leadership.* New York: Palgrave Macmillan, 2010.

Chernow, Ron. *Washington: A Life.* New York: Penguin Press, 2010.

Commager, Henry Steele and Richard B. Morris, eds. *The Spirit of 'Seventy-Six: The Story of the American Revolution as Told by Participants.* New York: Harper & Row, 1967.

Custis, George Washington Parke, and Mary Randolph Custis Lee. *Recollections and Private Memoirs of Washington.* Washington, D.C.: W.H. Moore, 1859.

Ellis, Joseph J. *His Excellency: George Washington.* New York: Alfred A. Knopf, 2004.

Fischer, David Hackett. *Washington's Crossing.* Oxford, England/ New York: Oxford University Press, 2004.

Fleming, Thomas. *Liberty!: The American Revolution.* New York: Viking, 1997.

Ketchum, Richard M. *The Winter Soldiers: The Battles for Trenton and Princeton.* New York: Henry Holt, 1999.

Lengel, Edward G. *General George Washington: A Military Life.* New York: Random House, 2005.

McCullough, David G. *1776.* New York: Simon & Schuster, 2005.

Scheer, George F. and Hugh F. Rankin, eds. *Rebels and Redcoats: The American Revolution Through the Eyes of Those Who Fought and Lived It.* New York: Da Capo Press, 1957.

Index

About the Author

Danny Kravitz is an Emmy award-winning writer and songwriter and a professor of screenwriting at Columbia College in Chicago. He has written for TV, film, and print media. Danny combines his passion for storytelling with his love of history. He is also a sports and nature enthusiast. He resides in Chicago, Illinois.